LETTER TRACING FOR KIDS

NORA

TRACE MY NAME WORKBOOK

Can't Find Your Name?

Have our elves create a personalized book with the name of your choice today!

VISIT US AT:
PersonalizeThisBook.com

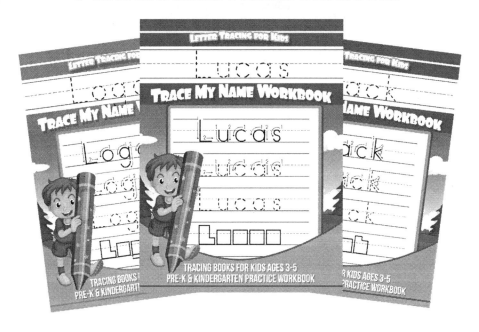

Chiquita publishing

Cover and page design by Cool Journals Studios - Copyright 2017

ABOUT ME

MY NAME IS:

Nora

I AM [ ] YEARS OLD.

I LIVE IN:

For parents

For kids

DRAW YOU AND YOUR FAMILY

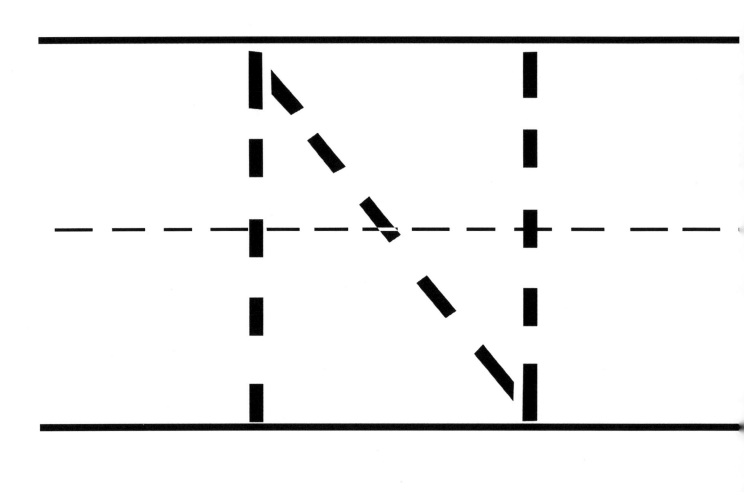

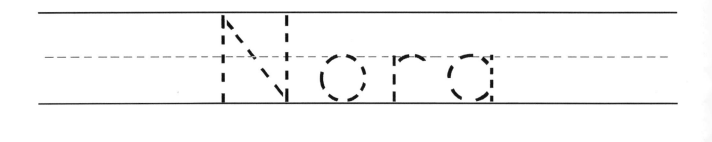

THIS IS HOW I WRITE MY NAME

MY NAME HAS ___ LETTERS

1	2	3	4	5	6	7	8

Nora

ora

ra

a

Nora

Nora

COLOR THE EGGS WITH LETTERS OF OUR NAME WRITE YOUR NAME

P B M F I
V T D E S
Z N L C J
R A Y Q W
G U K O H
X

WRITE YOUR NAME

Nora

WRITE YOU NAME WITH.

PEN

Nora

CRAYON

Nora

WRITE YOUR NAME IN BLUE

Nora

WRITE YOUR NAME IN YELLOW

Nora

DRAW YOUR FAVORITE THINGS

COLOR

FOOD

TOY

ANIMAL

MY NAME

MY NAME STARTS WITH	MY NAME ENDS WITH
_____	_____

FILL THE LETTERS OF YOUR NAME WHITH DIFFERENT COLORS

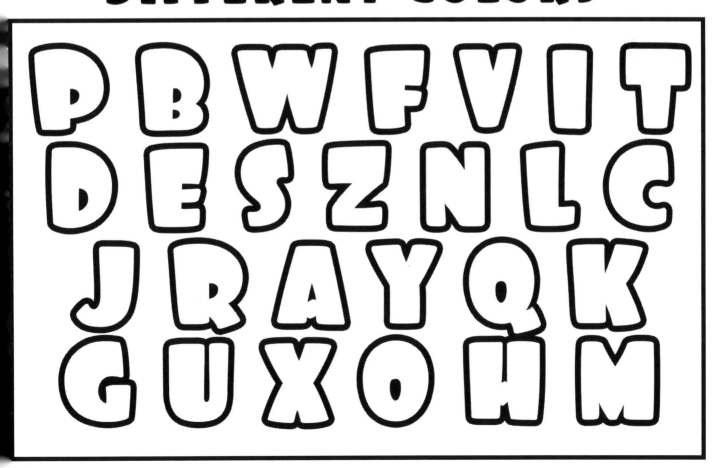

Nora

Nora

Nora

Nora

Nora

Nora

Nora

Nora

Nora

Nora

Nora

Nora

Nora

Nora

Nora

Nora

Nora

Nora

Nora

Nora

Nora

Nora

Nora

Nora

Nora

Nora

Nora

Nora

Nora

Nora

Nora

Nora

Nora

Nora

Nora

Nora

Nora

Nora

Nora

Nora

Nora

Nora

Nora

Nora

Nora

Nora

Nora

Nora

Nora

Nora

Nora

Nora

Nora

Nora

Nora

Nora

Nora

Nora

Nora

Nora

Nora

Nora

Nora

Nora

Nora

Nora

Nora

Nora

Nora

Nora

Nora

Nora

Nora

Nora

Nora

NNNN

NNNN

NNNN

NNNN

NNNN

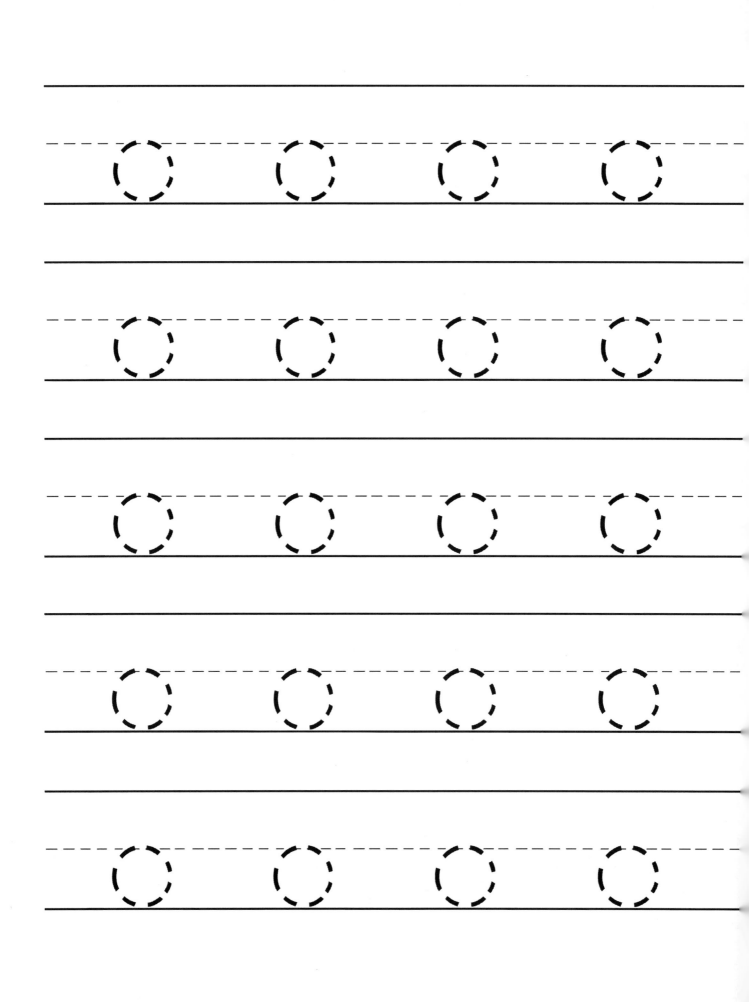

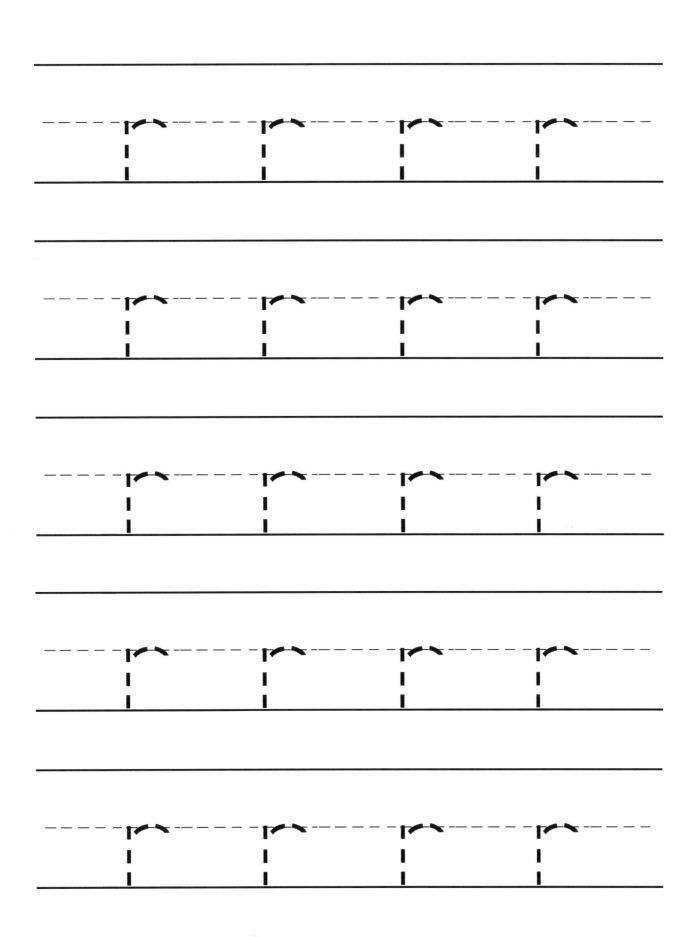

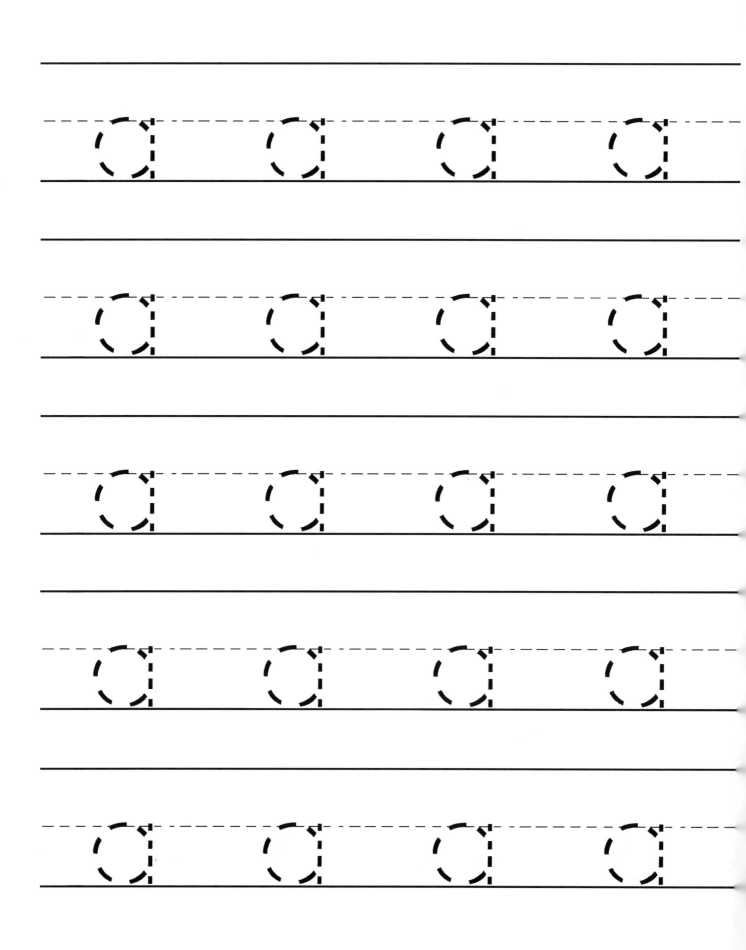

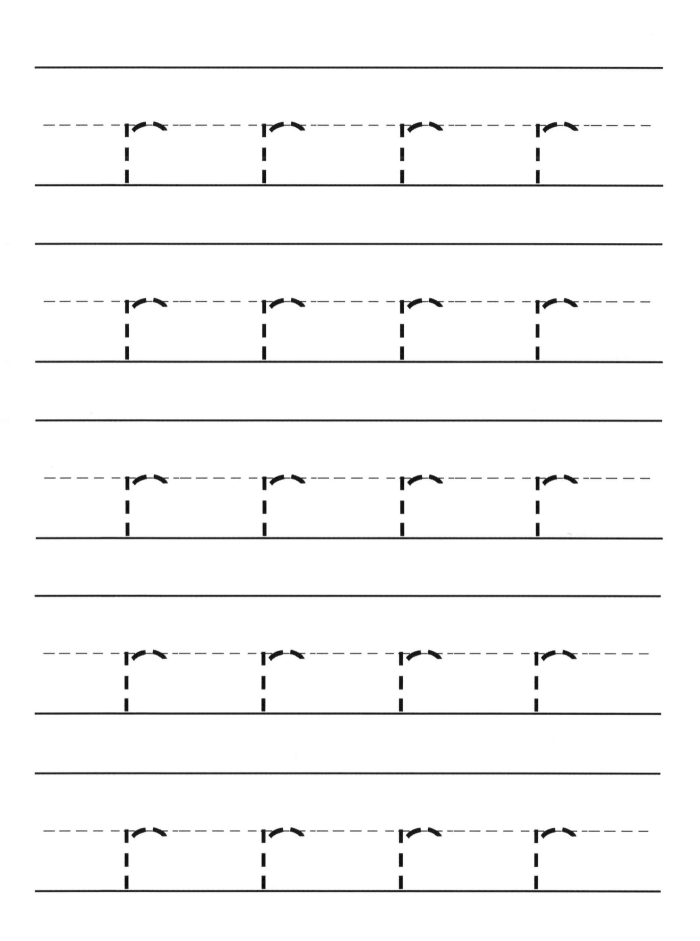

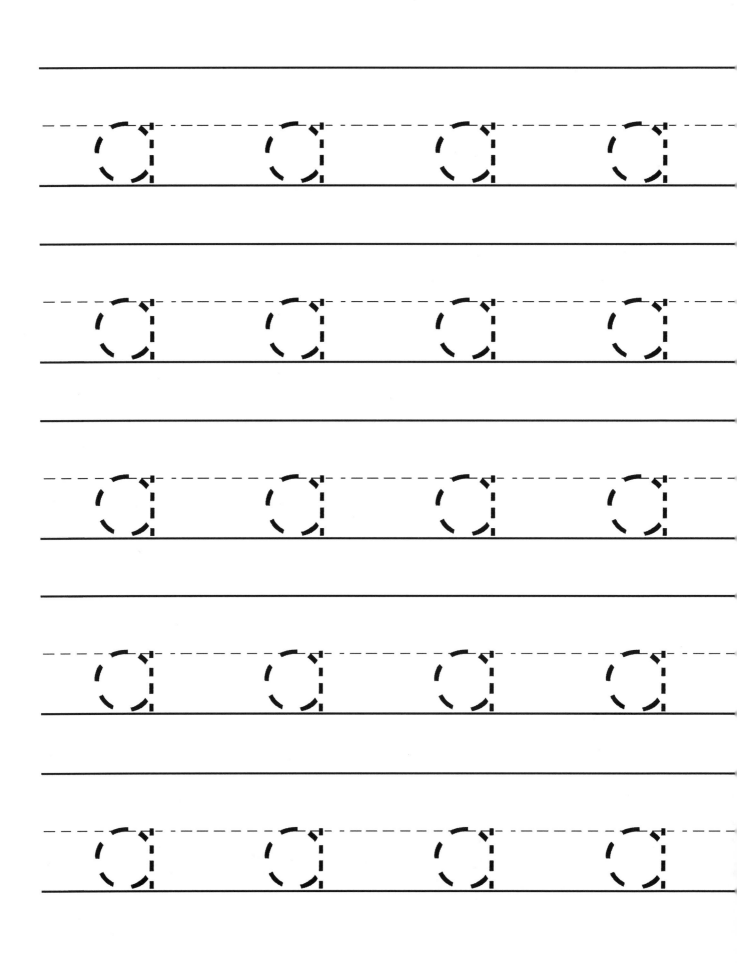

N N N N

N N N N

N N N N

N N N N

N N N N

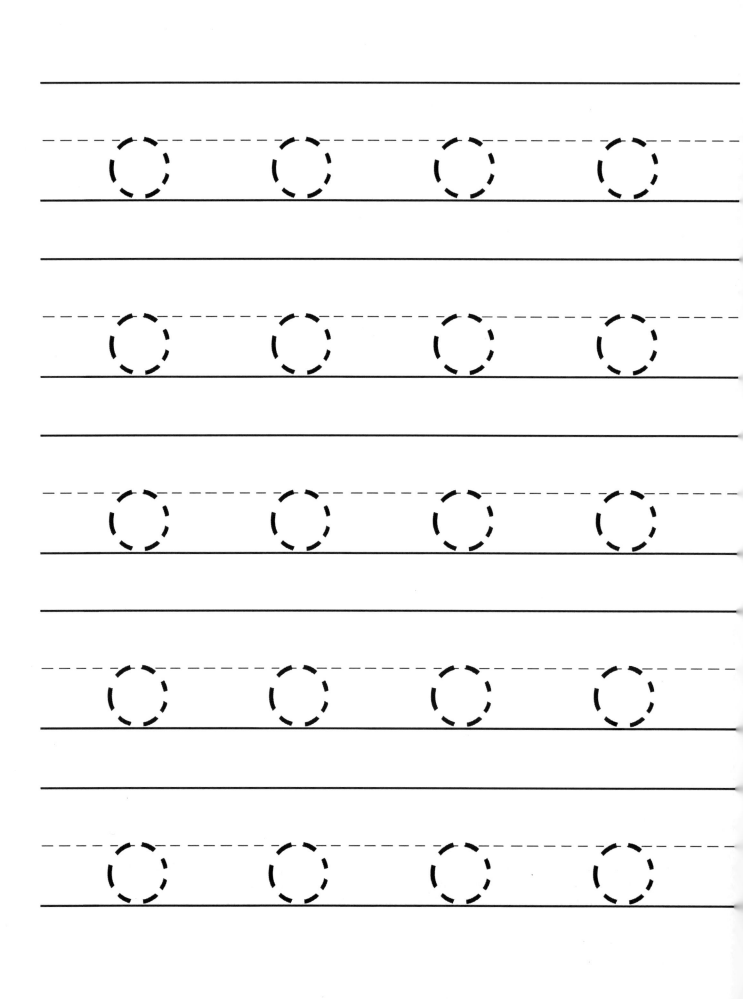

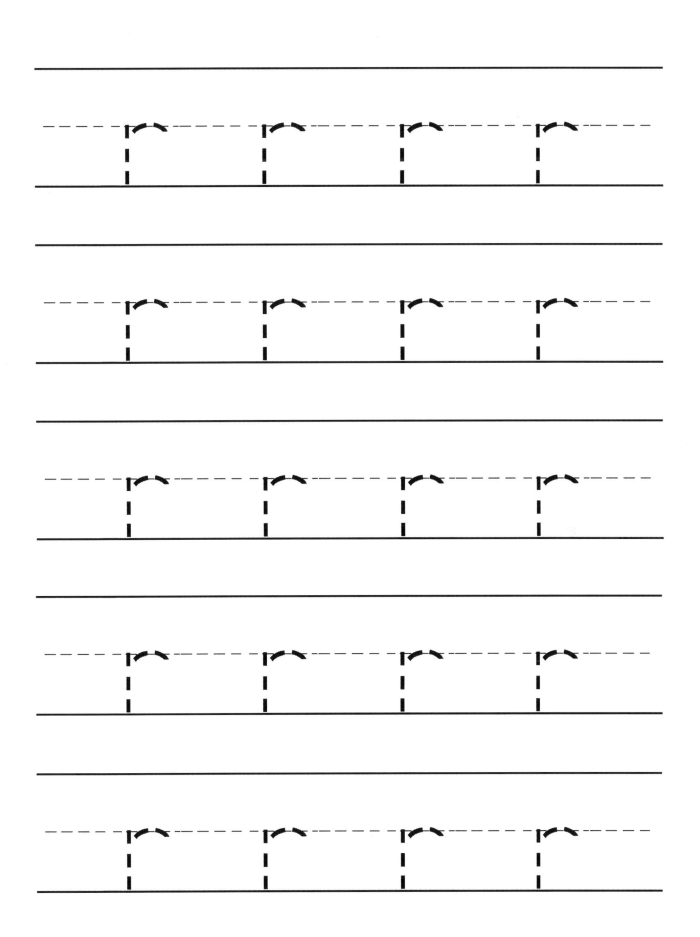

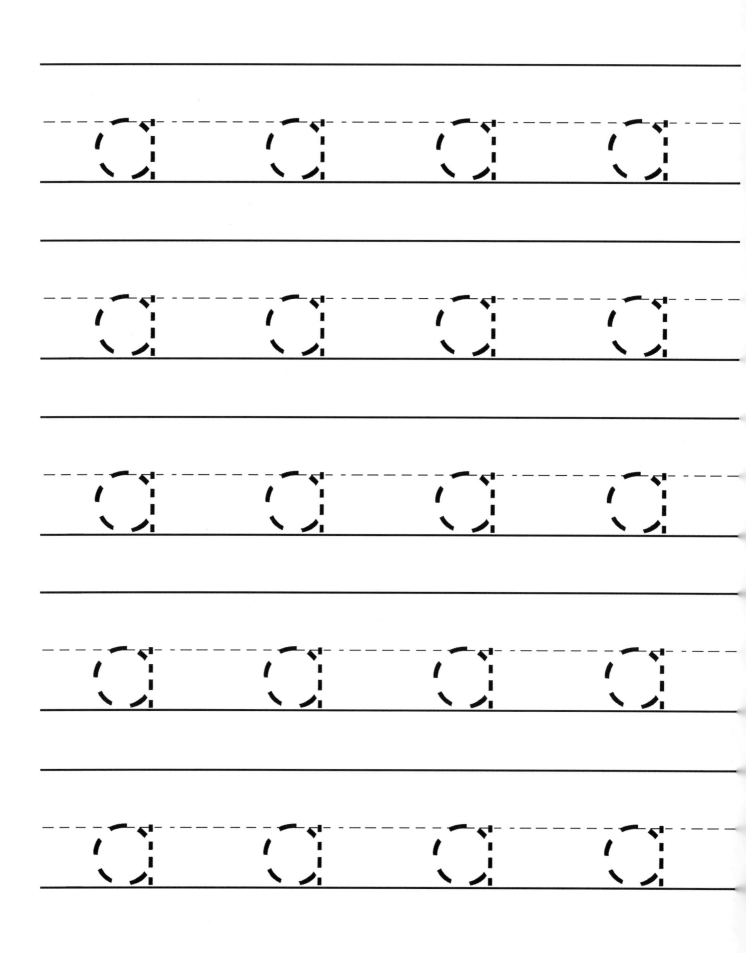

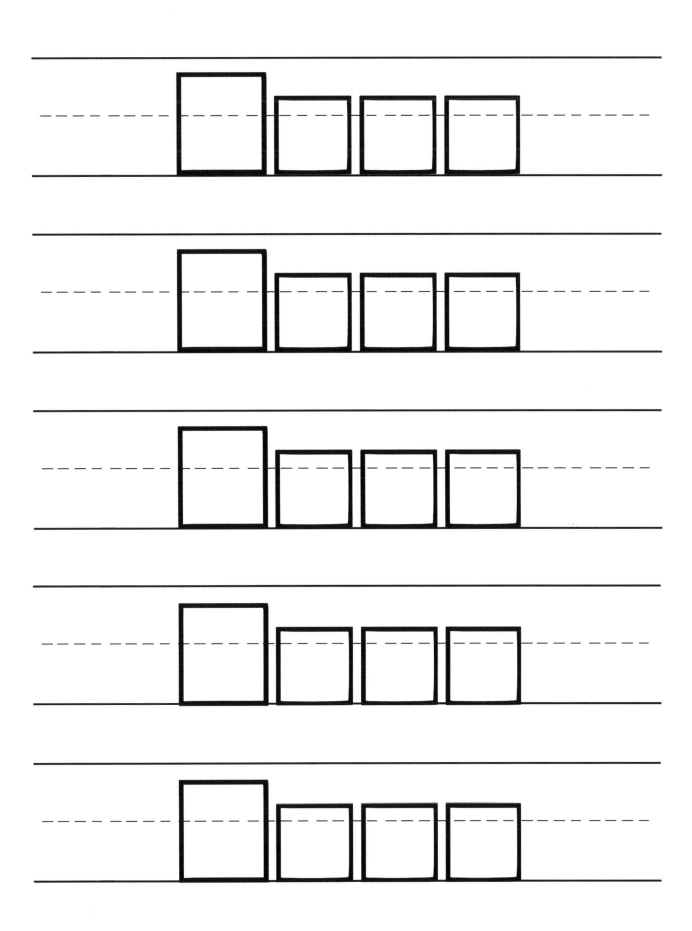

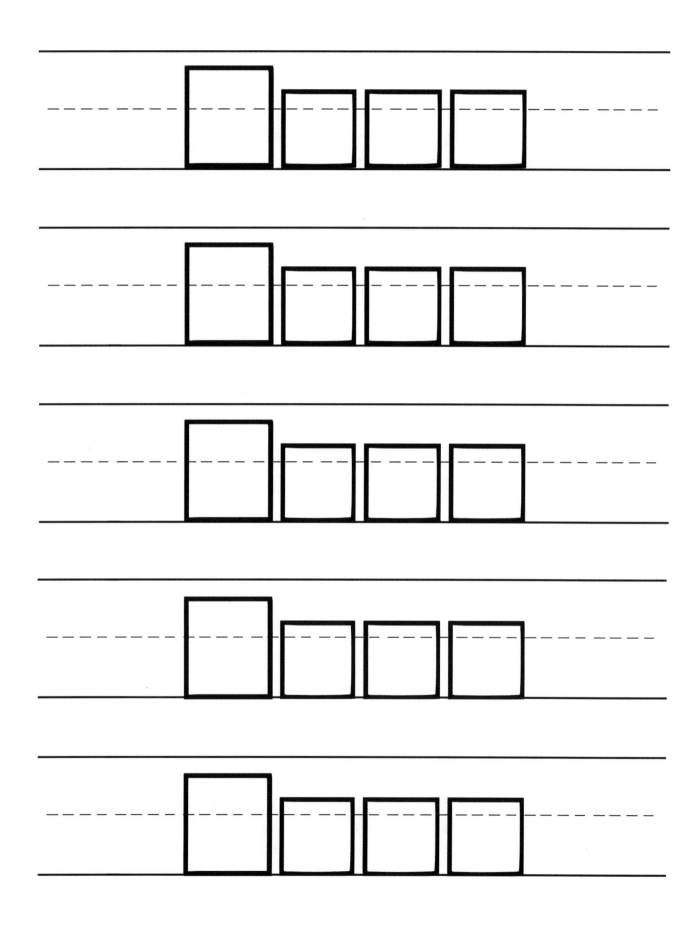

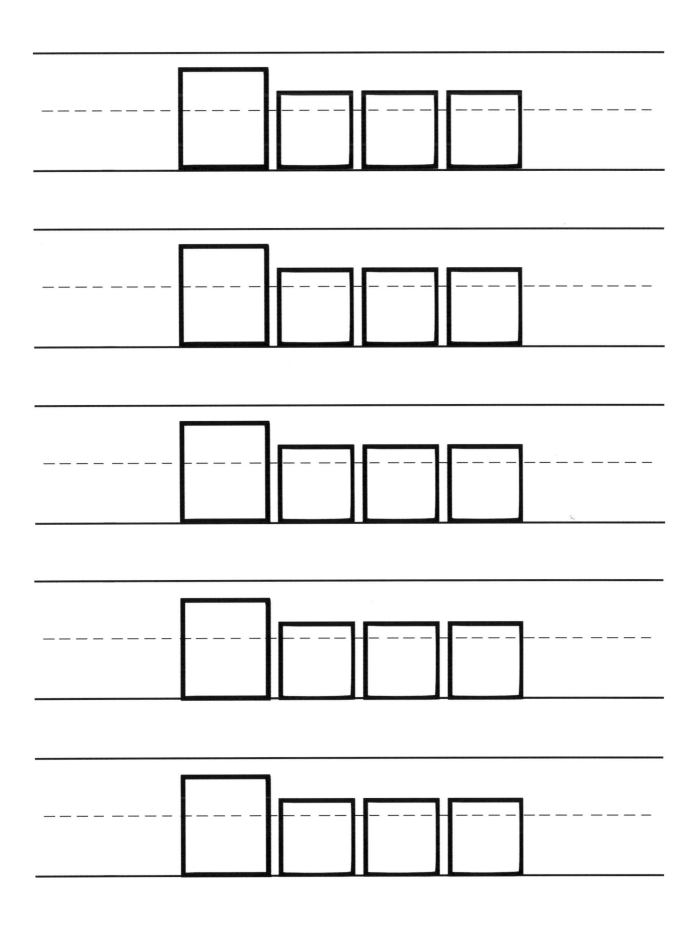

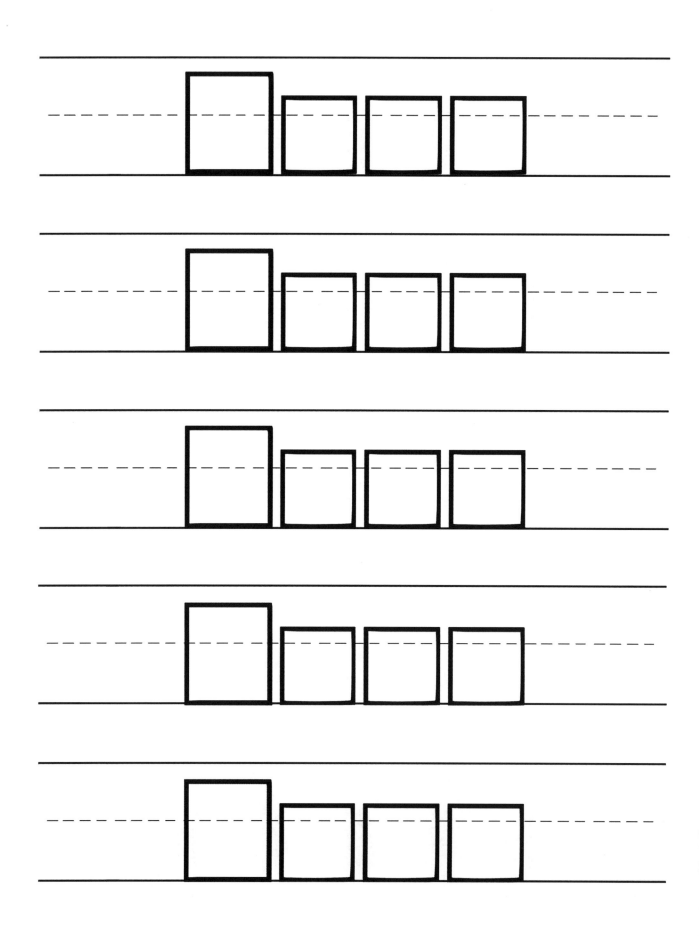

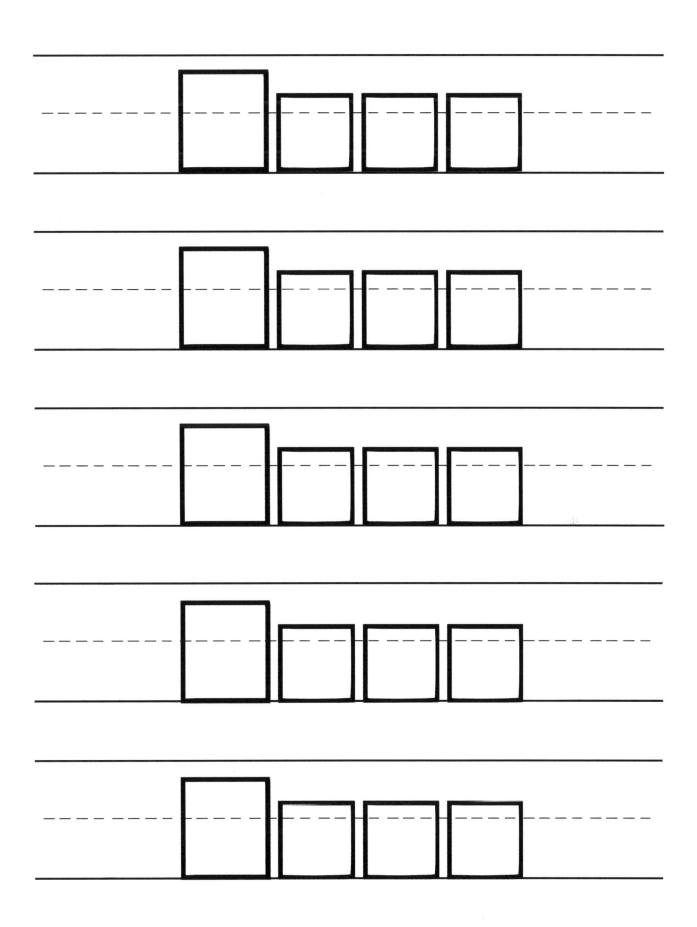

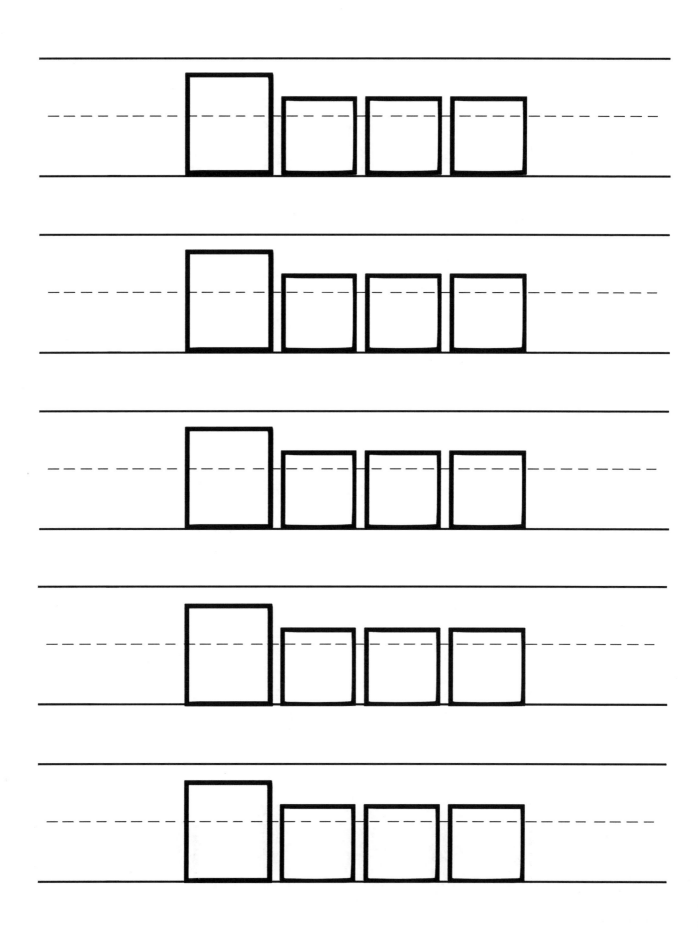

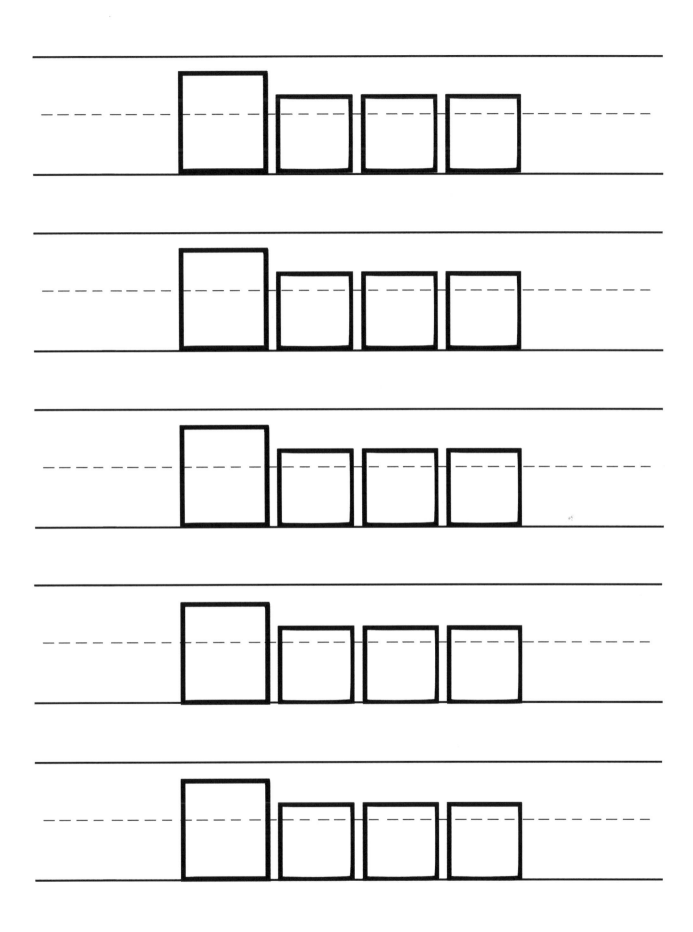

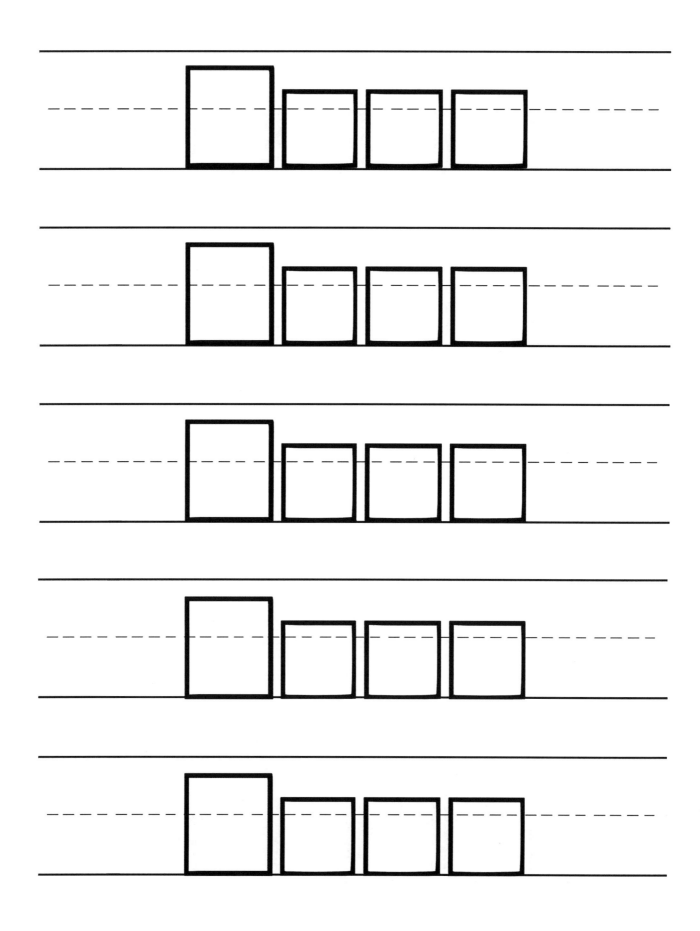

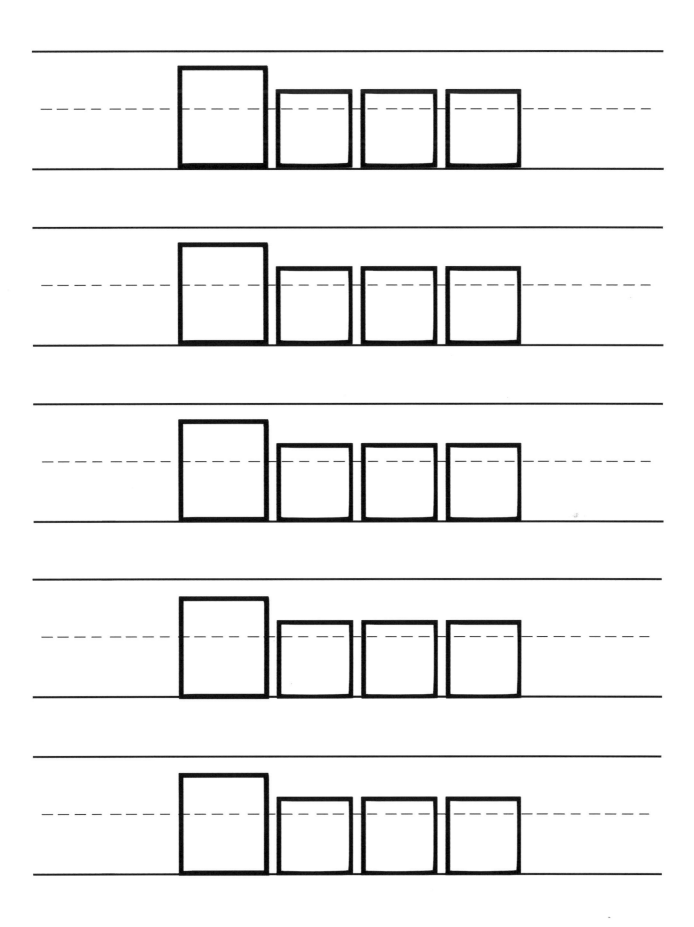

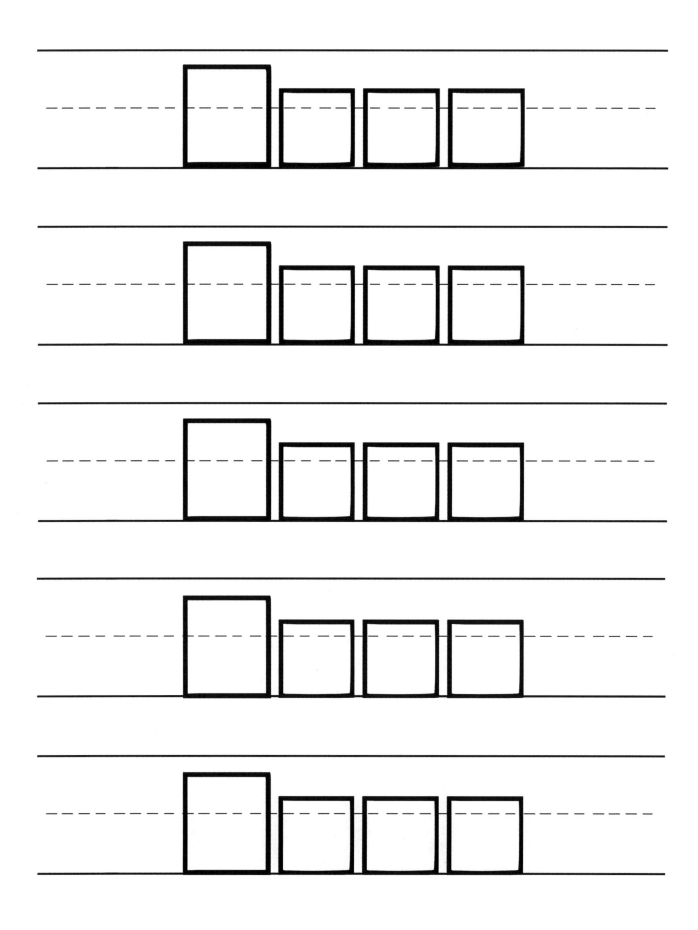

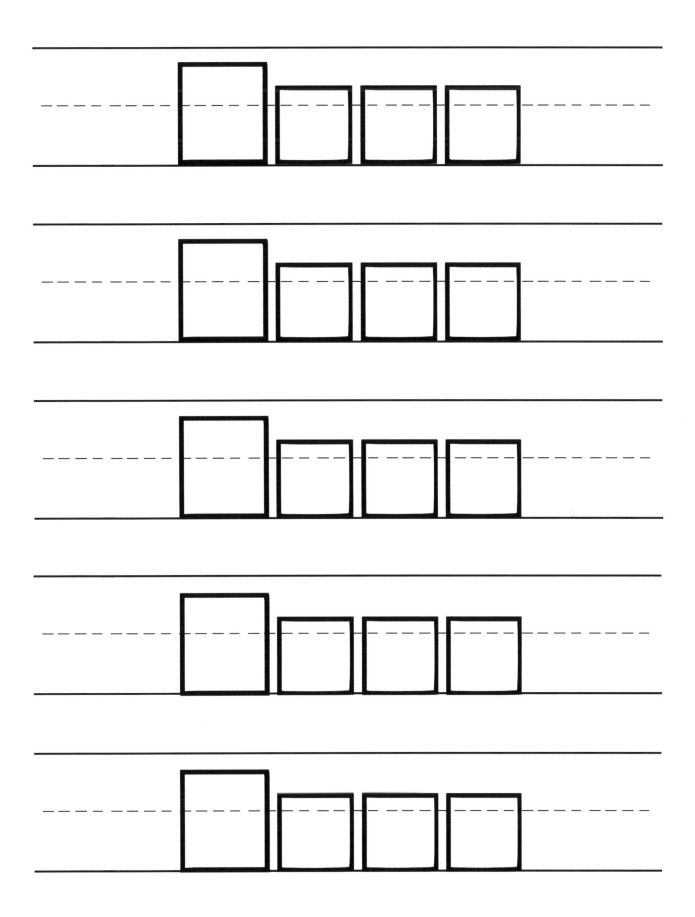

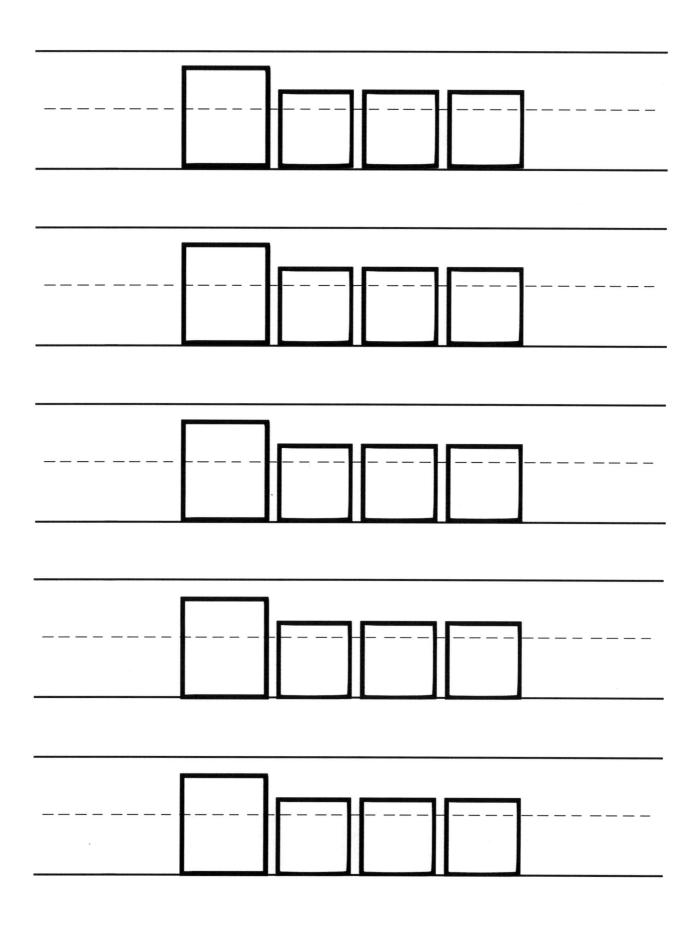

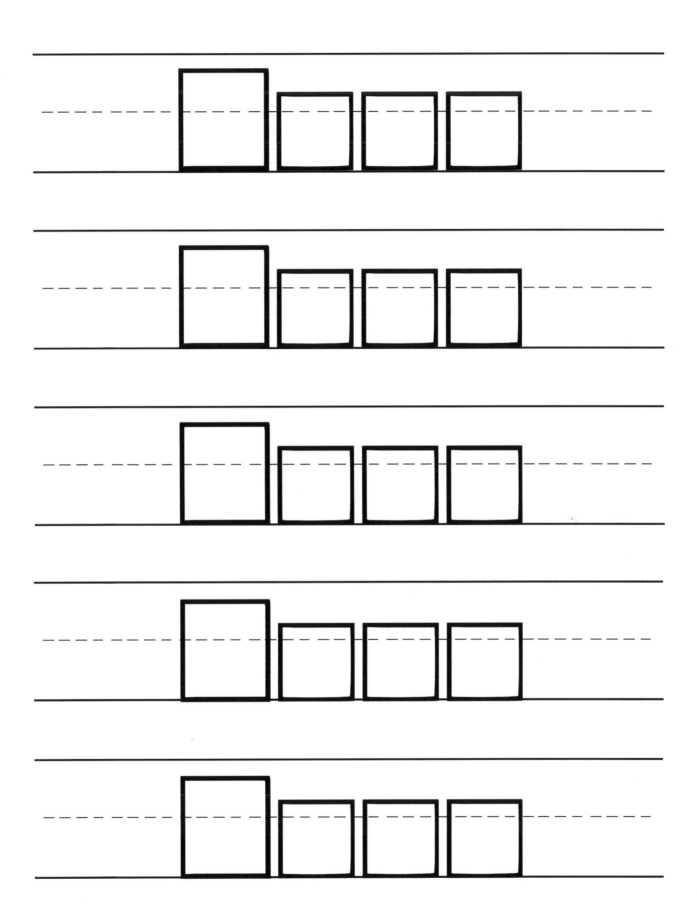

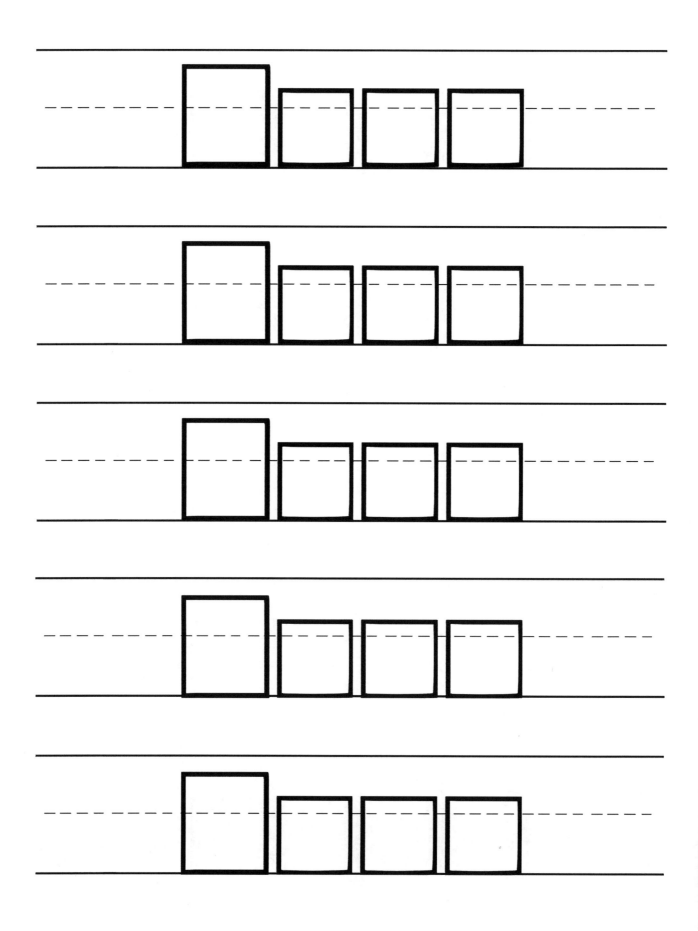

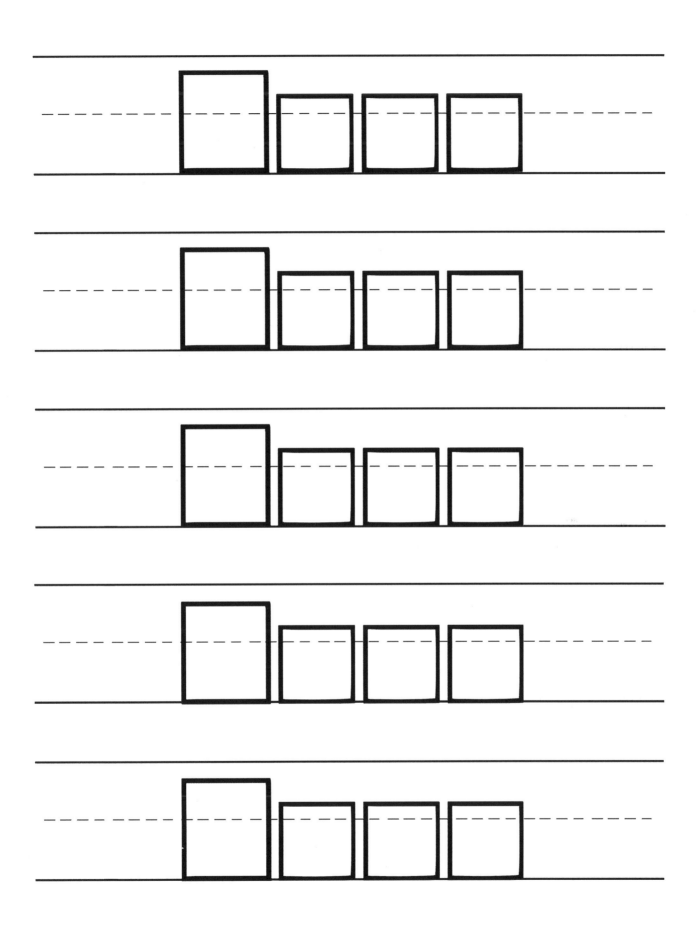

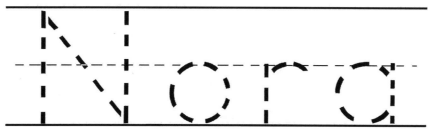

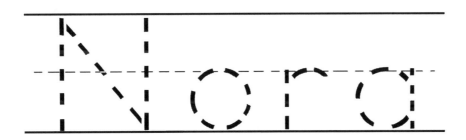

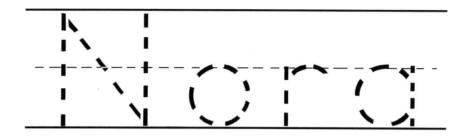

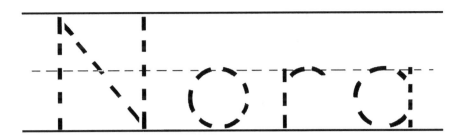

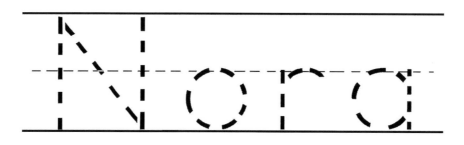

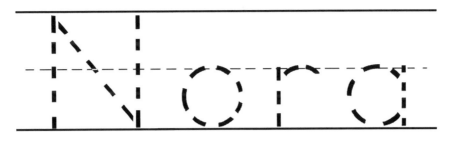

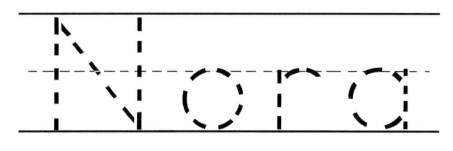

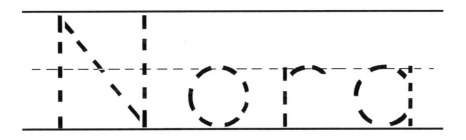

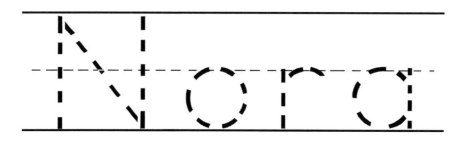

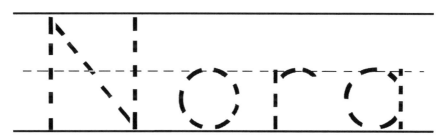

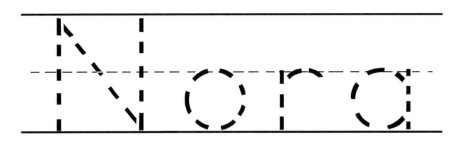

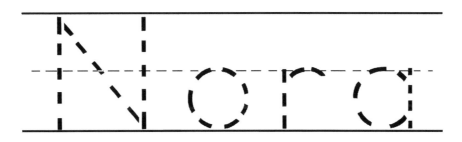

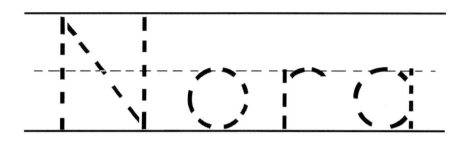

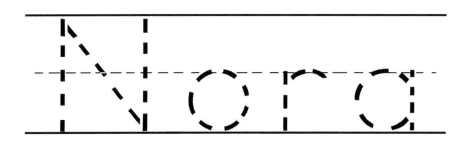

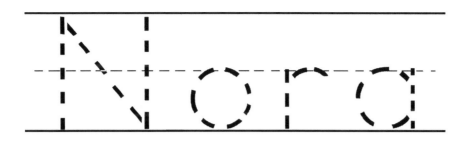

Nora

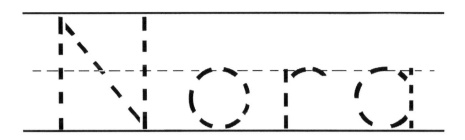

Nora

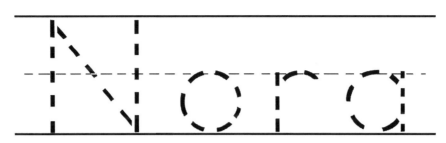

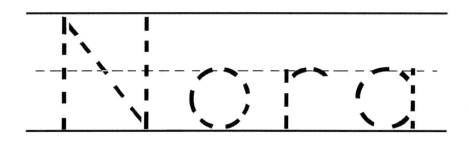

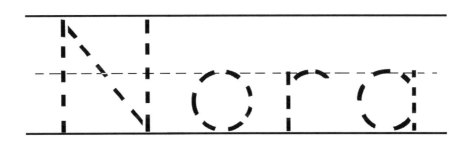

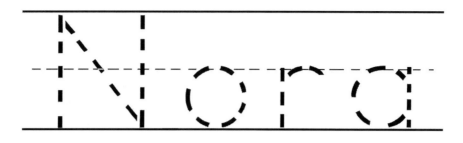

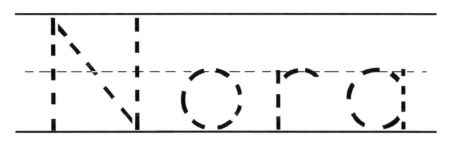

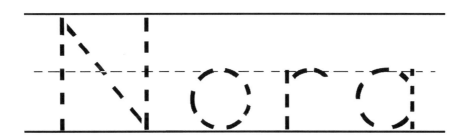

Nora

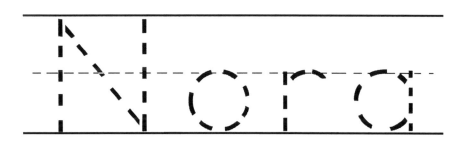

Nora

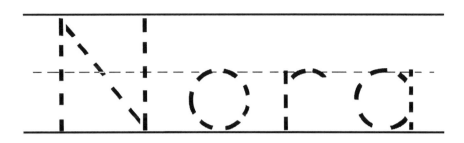

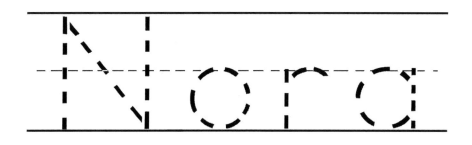

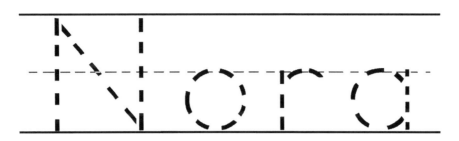

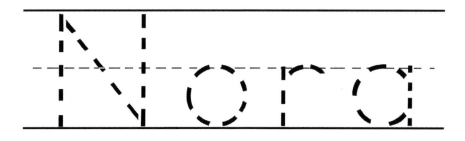

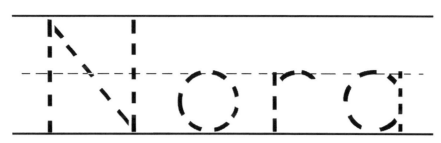

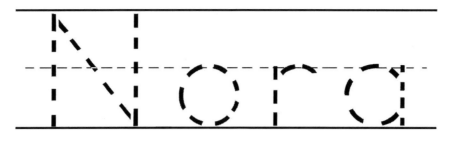

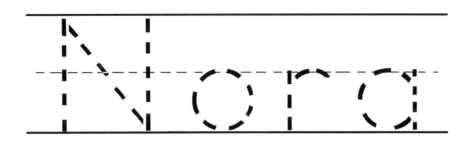

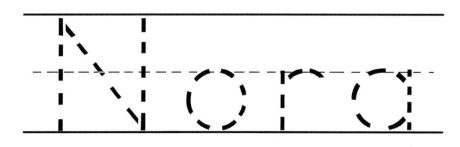

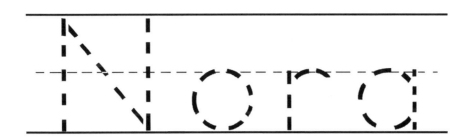

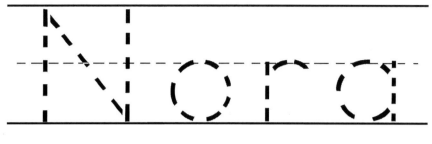

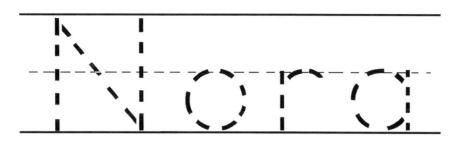

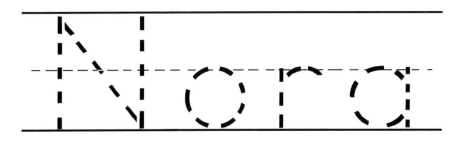

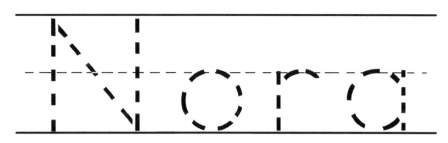

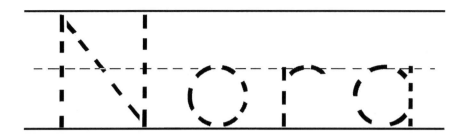

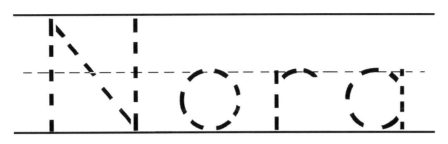

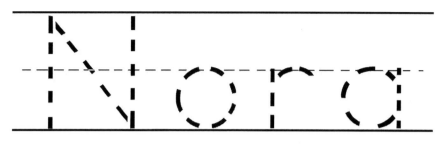

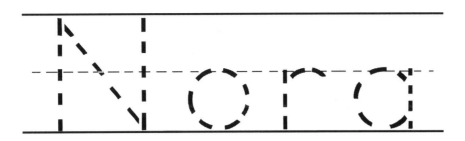

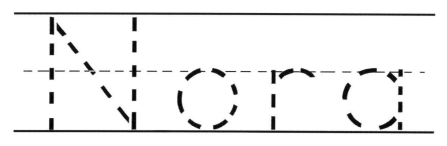

Made in the USA
Coppell, TX
19 November 2022